SELL YOUR BOOK, SCRIPT OR COLUMN

SELL YOUR BOOK, SCRIPT OR COLUMN

✦

How to Write a Winning Query and Make a Winning Pitch

Gini Graham Scott, Ph.D.

ASJA Press
New York Lincoln Shanghai

SELL YOUR BOOK, SCRIPT OR COLUMN
How to Write a Winning Query and Make a Winning Pitch

ASJA Press
an imprint of iUniverse, Inc.

iUniverse books may be ordered through booksellers or by contacting:

iUniverse
2021 Pine Lake Road, Suite 100
Lincoln, NE 68512
www.iuniverse.com
1-800-Authors (1-800-288-4677)

Because of the dynamic nature of the Internet, any Web addresses or links contained in this book may have changed since publication and may no longer be valid.

The views expressed in this work are solely those of the author and do not necessarily reflect the views of the publisher, and the publisher hereby disclaims any responsibility for them.

ISBN: 978-0-595-45009-1

Printed in the United States of America

Contents

INTRODUCTION

In today's digital age, decision-makers in various industries—publishing, films, music, toys and game, the media, venture capitalists, manufacturers, and more—are increasingly receptive to e-mail queries to open the door to considering your project. Rather than faxes, phone calls, and regular mail, this is the way to start the process. You can always use a postal query for the hold-outs.

However you do it, how you write your initial query is the key to success. This is what gets your e-mail query opened and read. Then, this initial impression shapes the way your project is considered.

This book is designed to help you write a powerful query letter, drawing on my experience of over four years of writing queries for over 900 clients, as well as writing my own queries for a series of services I set up to make connections. These services include:

- www.publishersandwriters.net—book publishers and agents and syndicates

- www.screenplaywritersconnection.com—the film industry

- www.songplaywritingconnection.com—the music industry

- www.venturecapitalconnection.com—venture capitalists

- www.newsmediaconnection.com—speaker bureaus, meeting planners and the media

- www.gameandtoyconnection.com—the game and toy industry

- www.thebusinessconnection.org—connecting with other businesses

- www.makingconnections.biz—connecting with any industry

In the following sections, I have included articles on writing good query letters, guidelines to write your own letter, and samples of letters I have written that led to high responses and resulted in deals in different industries. I have changed any identifying information in these letters.

The first section provides general tips on pitching your material, writing a good query, and formatting it for an e-mail query, which is different from sending a postal query. It includes some articles about whether to directly contact the publishers, editors, producers, and production companies or seek an agent to represent you. Or can you do both at the same time, and how? The next sections feature guidelines for writing a query for books, articles, columns, and screenplays. The basic principles are the same from industry to industry. Finally, the last section includes some sample letters, organized by industry.

You'll find this information invaluable in knowing how to best make that all important connection. Then, when you are ready to make those connections, our various services can help, since we have already done the hard work of identifying who to contact and we can make the connections quickly and efficiently, using our special software. In any case, whether you make your own connections or enlist our help, happy querying with a winning query letter!

Gini Graham Scott, Ph.D.

PART I
GETTING PREPARED

SHOULD YOU GET AN AGENT OR PITCH YOUR BOOK YOURSELF?

A question that frequently comes up for writers is whether to get an agent or pitch a book directly to editors and publishers. Ideally, if you have a commercial nonfiction or fiction book, it's ideal to get an agent—and an agent will want to represent you. In this ideal scenario, a good agent will have the connections and can place your book faster with a bigger and better publisher. Plus the agent can negotiate a bigger advance and better terms.

So how do you get to that agent? If you already have a high-profile, are involved in a big news event, or know people in the news and media, you can usually quickly connect up with an agent and even choose among eager agents.

Common Problems in Finding a Good Agent

Then there's everyone else—which is most writers with a book. Without that big name or big story connection, it is often difficult to find a good agent who is well connected in the industry and regularly making deals. You want to avoid an agent who charges fees other than out-of-pocket costs for copying and extra shipping, such as for foreign postage and messages.

One problem in finding representation is that good agents are often busy with other clients, are selective in taking on new clients, and may take weeks or months to respond. Then, too, some agents will only consider new clients by referral. So expect to encounter some of these common barriers to finding an agent, even if your book is one that an agent will be eager to represent.

Even after you get an agent, some common problems for many writers are these:

- the agent isn't doing enough;

- the agent has submitted the book to some editors, who have turned it down, and the agent isn't sure where to go next;

- an agent may be initially hot on a book, but after a few turn-downs, loses interest;

- an agent usually cultivates a select circle of editors—perhaps two or three dozen. But if those editors aren't interested, the agent has limited contacts or lacks an interest in pursuing your project outside the circle.

In such cases, getting or staying with an agent may not be the best approach. You may do better on your own.

Another consideration is whether your book is suited to a particular agent—or to agents, generally. While most agents handle general commercial nonfiction, many emphasize certain specialties or only handle certain types of books, such as fiction, children's book, self-help, health, and business books. Also, agents commonly submit most books to their circle of editors. So target your book to agents who handle your type of book.

Deciding If Your Book Is Better Suited to an Agent, Direct Pitching, or Both

While having a good agent is often the best approach, consider whether your book is best suited for an agent. Often, you will do better in pitching certain types of books yourself. In general, agents are best for books which have the potential for large sales, whether commercial nonfiction or fiction, or for special markets that have a big sales potential (such as popular psychology, self-help, and business books). In such cases, where big sales are possible, agents are ideal if you can find a good one, because they mostly focus on working with the bigger publishers who handle such books.

Conversely, if your book appeals to a specialty market or has limited sales potential, you might do better pitching your book directly to editors and publishers—or even think about self-publishing to launch your book. But only go the self-publishing route if you have the interest and ability to distribute books to your target market (such as if you are a speaker and can sell books in the back of the room). You need that commitment to distribution if you self-publish, because distribution is the hardest and most time-consuming part of self-publishing. The advantage of self-publishing, if suitable for you, is that once you establish a sales track record, you are in a stronger position to successfully pitch your book to a larger publisher.

Some types of books where you might do better with your own direct pitching include:

- specialized self-help books (such as on home improvements, buying a house, and saving on income tax)

- academic books (especially those most suited to university publishers)

- professional books (such as those mainly of interest to other professionals in your field, such as books for lawyers, doctors, and psychiatrists)

- business books (unless it's a book that will appeal to a broad general market as well as managers)

Commonly, specialty books have limited sales potential and are produced by special divisions in big houses or by small to medium publishers which specialize in a certain area. As a result, agents may often not show much enthusiasm for representing such books—or they may not know the small or medium publishers to contact, due to their focus on the larger publishers and more commercial books. By contrast, many small and medium publishers are used to dealing directly with writers; some even prefer to do so. They may not offer as big advances as the bigger publishers, because they don't have the budget; but they usually can publish your book more quickly—and they are often more receptive to your book than a larger publisher. So, in such cases, it's best to contact the publisher yourself.

When to Use a Dual Submission Approach

What if you are not sure about the potential for your book? One good approach then is to look for an agent and a publisher at the same time, and refer any interested publishers to an agent, if you find an agent you want to work with. That's an approach I often use myself. I send out queries about book projects to editors several times a year, and have several agents representing me on different books. Should any of these mailings result in a lead for a book where I have an agent, I turn the lead over to that agent to follow-up. Typically the arrangement I have is that the agent gets 71/2-10% where I supply the lead, depending on the type of book, instead of the usual 15% when the agent does it all.

When you use this dual approach, tell any agent you contact about any publishers who have expressed interest. Sometimes just getting this interest can help you get an agent, who will then contact other publishers, building on what you started. Alternatively, try initially querying the smaller and medium sized publishers, while you look for an agent, since some agents will prefer to contact the bigger publishers themselves. This way, you can explore two avenues at the same time—either finding a smaller or medium-sized publisher or obtaining an agent who will pursue the larger publishers. Once you do get an agent, turn over any leads to that agent; or if you don't get an agent, try contacting editors at the larger publishers yourself, if you think your book might appeal to a wide audience; or go with a smaller or medium sized publisher, who has already shown an interest in your book.

In short, there are times when it's better to seek an agent and times when it's better to do it yourself, though often you don't know what to do, particularly when you don't know if an agent will be interested or respond quickly enough. That's when the best choice may be a dual approach, where you test out the waters to see whether you can find an agent, or whether it may be better to work with a smaller or medium-sized publisher.

HOW TO GET A GOOD AGENT

Are you having trouble finding a good agent you like working with? If so, join the club. This is one of the most common complaints of writers, including long-time professional writers. Even writers who have an agent may be looking for another one, or have different types of writing projects better handled by another agent.

This article will help you find and select an agent, including how to best contact an agent initially and how to follow-up with additional information.

Selecting an Agent

Some considerations to keep in mind when choosing the agent that's best for you are:

- <u>Types of books handled</u>. Most agents handle multiple types of books, but some agents specialize. It can be useful to choose an agent who handles several types of books if you have different types of writing projects. Or you may prefer to divide up different types of books with different agents, if the agents agree. In some cases, agents will handle other types of projects for clients, but only when they are representing the client for their primary area of emphasis. (Most commonly this occurs when the agent represents you for non-fiction and additionally takes on fiction, children's books, or scripts). Check on what types of manuscripts the agent handles to decide what's best for you.

- <u>Film and TV rights</u>. Most agents handle film and TV rights for projects they represent—generally through a rep in L.A. or elsewhere on the West Coast, though some handle the rights themselves. If you want an agent who specializes in film and TV rights, look for one who is a member of the Writers Guild of America (WGA), since many producers, production companies, and studios will only deal with WGA agents. You can find these agents listed on the WGA Web site, and the Hollywood Creative Directory at <u>www.hcdonline.com</u> also has a directory which comes out twice a year which features agents and managers.

- <u>Foreign reps and rights.</u> Most agents handle foreign rights, generally through a subagent or group of subagents, although some handle these rights themselves. Should you want to know the foreign reps which different agents use, the listings for many agents are in the <u>Literary Marketplace</u>, which is available in a hard copy which comes out annually and online.

- <u>Location.</u> Decide if you prefer an agent who is near you or who is near the publishers, if you live out of the major publishing centers. These are in New York City (especially for mainstream commercial books), Los Angeles (especially for film and TV projects), and the San Francisco Bay Area (especially for more targeted smaller audience and independent books). Generally, it is best to get an agent in the major centers, especially in New York, New Jersey, Connecticut, Massachusetts, and Washington, D.C. on the East Coast or in California on the West Coast. Within these states, it is best to have an agent who is close to the major publishing centers. Still, many agents do extensive traveling and some have relocated from these centers, so they may still be well connected. Then, too, if you like having face-to-face contact with your agent, you may prefer one in your area.

- <u>Size of Agency.</u> While many agents are independent or work in small agencies, others are part of large agencies or affiliations of agents, such as William Morris, International Creative Management, and Writers House. While a big name affiliation can help new agents gain clout, many independent agents or agents in smaller agencies have excellent reputations and have sold big books. While you can initially query more than one agent in an agency, since not all agents will be interested in the same project, if more than one expresses interest, you have to decide which one to follow-up with additional material. To explain why you contacted more than one agent in the same agency, you can say that you weren't sure who to contact. This multiple contact approach works better when you are sending e-mails, since this is a more informal type of initial contact. If you are sending a query by regular mail, it is better to pick one agent in an agency to query first. Then, if you have no response from that agent in a couple of weeks, try a second agent at that agency.

- <u>Affiliations and Listings.</u> An agent's affiliations and listings in directories of agents can help you decide whom to contact, too. The agents who are listed in <u>Literary Marketplace</u> and/or are members of the Association of Authors' Representatives (AAR) generally have fairly solid credentials, although the AAR list provides little information other than whether an agent handles nonfic-

tion, fiction, children's books, or dramatic works. A number of popular directories include more detailed information on some of these agents. But many of
the bigger and more established agents aren't listed in these directories or don't
provide much information, since they get most of their new clients by referrals
or through industry sources, like panel discussions of agents for writers groups.
Still you can often break through to a big agent with a well-written query
about a compelling project. The PublishersAndAgents Agent Assessment and
Location Service also provides some detailed information on agent affiliations.

- Areas of Specialization. Besides the broad areas of specialization—Nonfiction
(N), Fiction (F), Scripts/Screenplays (S), and Children's Books (which range
from juveniles to young adults) (C)—many agents and agencies describe their
interests in various sources. Where these descriptions are available, you can
find agents or agencies with particular interests (i.e. "business" if you have a
business book; "self-help" or "relationships" if you have a personal improve-
ment book). However, don't overlook the agents who don't provide such
information, since many agents who haven't listed the particular subject area
of your book or haven't listed any specialties may still be interested, especially
if your book is a general trade or commercial nonfiction or fiction book.

- Reputation. A big concern of writers is whether an agent is truly reputable.
Generally, you can trust agents you learn about through a personal referral, an
appearance on industry panels, or a referral by other writers who have been
published or are members of professional writers' organizations. Another good
source for reputable agents is Publishers Marketplace, which lists the agents
involved in making deals each week (in fact, PublishersAndAgents has been
tracking these agents for over 2 years and has a record of the number and size
of deals made by these agents). A good way to eliminate agents who might be a
problem is to not contact agents who charge reading fees or promote editing
services (unless they do this on a limited basis for new, unpublished writers,
and also represent established writers at no charge). However, many agents do
charge fees for copying manuscripts, foreign calls, messengers, and postage,
and some ask for an advance retainer of about $50-200 to cover such costs, so
this isn't necessarily a warning sign. This request for fees is most common for
agents on the West Coast and outside of the main publishing centers, because
they have higher postage and phone expenses.

Sending Queries to Agents

At one time the best way to initially query an agent was by regular mail with an
SASE to get a response. But today most agents are receptive to initial e-mail queries, and if they express interest, you can follow-up with more information by e-

mail or regular mail, depending on the agent's preferences. However, don't send any attachments unless you get permission, since many people won't open attachments due to problems with viruses, unless the e-mail is from someone they know and the e-mail specifies what the person is sending. What works best—and what is most likely to get through the various spam filters today is a simple text message without any special graphics or photos.

As for phone queries, the vast majority of agents don't want them, with a few exceptions. And almost universally, agents don't want unsolicited manuscripts. So don't send the full manuscript unless it's requested, and this way, you keep your costs down, too, since copying and mailing manuscripts is expensive. The only exception is if you are writing short picture books, since most agents invite you to send it with a postal query.

Agents vary widely in what they want to review—ranging from a synopsis to a few chapters to a full manuscript. Since it is not always certain what agents want and whether they are open to new clients, a good way to make a first contact is to start with an initial query letter in which you include a brief description about your project and yourself and any past publications and PR. If you send this by e-mail, you will typically hear back with 1-2 days, sometimes within hours.

If you are initially sending a postal query, you can include a few additional pages, such as a synopsis and press clips. If the agents are interested, they can ask for more. This approach cuts down on your expenses of sending more detailed full proposals or outlines and chapters on the first round, so you only send these additional materials to agents who request them. This preliminary query approach also avoids the problem of sending your material to an agent who wants an exclusive look to consider it (typically asking for about 2-4 weeks to do this) until you have an initial show of interest.

Another advantage of an initial brief query is it enables you to send out multiple queries quickly and at little expense. This multiple query approach also increases your chances of finding an agent and choosing among those who are interested in your project, since agents commonly have a high rejection rate—about 95-98% for many agents, and some agents who show interest could be very busy and over-extended. Thus, with multiple agents expressing interest at this early stage, you can be more selective in whom to follow-up with by sending additional information.

Sending More Information to Interested Agents

Once an agent has expressed interest to your initial query, the agent typically wants to see certain basic materials. While different agents may have slightly different requests in what they want, generally, agents want to see the following materials, which are what they would send to a publisher if they represent you. So have these materials prepared and ready to go on request.

An advantage of creating this basic package is you have the information that most agents will want—and you can add or subtract materials from this basic package depending on the agent's requests.

For Nonfiction—Have a proposal which includes:

> Table of Contents
> Overview of the book
> Chapter by chapter outline, with brief descriptions for each chapter
> 1-3 sample chapters (up to about 50 pages)
> Description of the market
> Your bio, including your credentials for writing the book, and
> any promotional support you can provide

For Fiction—Have the following:

> Brief synopsis
> 1-3 sample chapters (typically 10-50 pages)
> Then be ready to send the whole manuscript on request

For Children's Books:

> For younger children: send the whole picture book
> (if you didn't already send it with your query letter).
> For older children: follow the non-fiction or fiction guidelines

For Scripts and Screenplays:

> Send a treatment if it's based on a book (you can adapt a detailed chapter by chapter outline to create this)
> Send the full script in standard script format if it's an original script.

WHAT YOU NEED TO SUBMIT YOUR BOOK TO EDITORS AND AGENTS

If you are seeking a publisher or agent to represent you, it all starts with an initial query to open the door. At one time, you normally had to send queries by regular mail and include a self-addressed stamped envelope (SASE). But now, the vast majority of editors and agents are open to e-mail queries, and if in interested in seeing more, many will accept proposals and manuscripts by e-mail attachments. Commonly, though, you will need to send additional material by regular mail.

To begin the process, start with a short query letter to briefly describe your manuscript and yourself. This letter is critical. You have to make your case in about 300-500 words for the agent or editor to want to see more. This pitch letter may be a different type of writing than you are used to. It is more akin to copywriting or writing a marketing letter selling your project. It's what will get the agent or editor to want to know more. Moreover, you need a compelling subject line to get the recipient to open your letter.

When you send out this initial query letter, be ready to follow through within 1-2 weeks, and preferably within a day or two, with the materials you need to sell your manuscript. If these aren't ready, wait until they are before sending your query, unless you are using the query to determine if there is enough interest to write your book. In that case, you can gage the level of interest by the response—but be sure to tell the interested agents or editors your plans and when they might expect your proposal or manuscript.

Assuming you have gotten interest, what do you need?

- If it's a nonfiction book, you need a proposal with the following sections:

- an overview, which should include the following:

  - a brief introduction to the book,

  - description of your primary audience,

  - a description of the market and how your book differs from the competition,

  - a bio of yourself, particularly as it relates to the book,

  - a brief explanation of why you are well suited to write the book and a description of your platform and how you are able to help promote and market the book.

  - a brief plan for the book, describing how long it will take you to write the book and any special needs for writing it.

- a chapter by chapter outline, with a short description of what's in each chapter.

- 1-2 sample chapters, showing your writing style. These can be an introduction and the first or second chapter; or choose the one or two strongest chapters in the book.

- Even if you have self-published a book, you need a brief proposal to provide a context for your book. If you have any significant sales figures, emphasize these; if not, it may be better to treat this as a non-published book, since limited sales might be a negative, unless you can explain why you had few sales.

- In brief, your proposal should include the following:

  - Table of Contents

  - Overview of the book

  - Chapter by chapter outline, with brief descriptions for each chapter

  - 1-3 sample chapters (50-80 pages)

  - Description of the market

  - Your bio, including your credentials for writing the book and any promotional support you can provide

  - Your plan for completing the book

- If it's a fiction book, you need a 1-2 page synopsis and at least two or three chapters, starting from the beginning of the book. Then, unless you have published a novel before, you normally need to have completed the book, so be prepared to send the complete manuscript on request. (Sometimes agents or editors will just want to see a synopsis and a few chapters to start; but if interested, they will ask for more. In other cases, they will ask for the full manuscript at the outset.) Additionally, include bio information and material on how you can help promote and market the book.

- If it's a children's books, use the following guidelines:

  - For younger children: send the whole picture book (if you didn't already send it with your query letter).

  - For older children: follow the nonfiction or fiction guidelines

Before you send anything, find out whether you can send your material as an e-mail attachment (usually as a PDF or Word document) or whether the editor or agent wants you to send the material by regular mail. Then, follow those guidelines.

In the event you have a Web site, an alternative is to post a link to a PDF or Word document or to both on a private page on your site and send the agent or editor the link. Then, offer downloading or viewing this online as an alternative to an e-mail attachment or regular mail. I have found that posting material on my Web site is a very convenient, time-saving way to submit material, since I just have to send the link to the Web page, and most agents and editors are receptive to this approach, but not all are. So you have to ask for their preference and do whatever the agent or editor prefers.

HOW TO PITCH YOUR BOOK TO EDITORS AND PUBLISHERS

While the ideal is to have a good agent to help you find a publisher for your book and negotiate the best possible contract, you can pitch your book to many editors yourself—and sometimes even help an agent who needs help. Another benefit of do-it-yourself pitching is that once you get an interested publisher, that can open the doors to finding an agent who can take over from there.

As a general rule, if you are writing nonfiction, start with a proposal; if you are writing fiction, complete the whole manuscript. In both cases, start with a query letter by e-mail or regular mail. Most are now receptive to an e-mail query done right, so that can be a good way to start; then you can send a regular query to those who don't accept e-mails or don't respond to an e-mail query. In your query, describe the project and why you are in a good position to write and help the publisher market and promote your book.

When to Look for an Editor or Publisher Yourself

There are a number of times when you may prefer to go it alone:

- <u>You have a specialized book for a limited market</u> (ie: a travel guide, history of China, or report of a new psychological treatment) and the book would have the most appeal to a niche publisher (ie: a publisher of travel books or an academic or professional publisher). An agent may not be interested in specialty books, since agents primarily focus on the mainstream commercial market. So if yours is such a book, you are generally better off finding the publisher yourself, and then you might negotiate the final contract, too, perhaps with the help of a lawyer who handles intellectual property or with an agent to do this, generally for a smaller than usual percentage (typically 7 ½-10%).

- <u>You have a book that you think has broad appeal, but you don't have an agent</u>. There could be any number of reasons for not having an agent—you have queried agents, but no one has responded; you don't know who to contact; you just fired an agent who didn't actively pitch your book; you are between agents. Whatever your reason, you might do better by pitching your book directly, particularly if it's a timely book that will lose its appeal if you wait to find an agent. Then, once you gain an editor's interest, you can use that to attract an agent and ask that agent to follow-up for you.

- <u>You have an agent who has been handling your book, but your agent needs help</u>. In this case, you might do better with another agent, or maybe your otherwise enthusiastic agent just needs some leads from you. Commonly, this problem of an agent not knowing where to go next occurs, because agents have their own stable of editors to contact. But after that group of editors has turned down your book, your agent may not know where to go next. But once you make the initial contact, you set the stage for your agent to handle the follow-up. Whatever the reason, once you decide to contact editors and publishers yourself, here's how to do it.

<u>Deciding What Types of Editors and Publishers To Contact</u>

A first critical step is assessing your manuscript to better target the appropriate publishers and editors. Smaller and mid-sized publishers will usually have a more limited area of focus, and editors are more likely to handle different types of books in this area, though some editors will have their own specialties. By contrast, in the bigger publishing houses, there are generally many imprints or divisions, and editors are often more specialized. So selectively target your queries to those editors who will be most likely to be interested in your type of book.

While you can't know precisely what a particular house or editor may want at any particular time, since interests change with events and publishers can change their focus, you can narrow down your contact list by thinking of your book in a series of general categories. Then look for editors and publishers who fall in those categories. The major categories include these:

<u>Nonfiction</u>: The major categories here include: general/commercial nonfiction (which includes memoirs, personal narratives, true crime), business, self-help/how-to (which includes books on popular psychology, health, fitness, and spirituality), pop culture/social issues/contemporary events, humor, illustrated books, academic books, and professional books.

<u>Fiction</u>: The major categories here include: general/commercial fiction, literary fiction, women's fiction/romance, mystery/suspense/thrillers, and science fiction/fantasy.

If you are looking for an agent while you are seeking a publisher, look for an agent who handles books in your area.

Another consideration in deciding what publishers to contact is the size of the publisher. While most everyone dreams of big mega-deals with the biggest publishers, only a relatively small number of books get this treatment—usually the high-profile celebrity and big news books that are expected to get big sales. Often the process of producing these books is speeded up, so what usually takes many months in the normal editorial process in the big houses occurs in a matter of weeks. As a result, a book can come out in a month rather than a more usual 12 to 18 months from contract signing time in the bigger houses (plus 2-3 months to make a decision). By contrast, the smaller publishers usually make decisions and bring out books much faster—in about 6-9 months, but the advances are typically lower—about $1000-5000 or even nothing versus $8000-20,000 for the average book in the bigger houses. (The 6-figure and million-dollar deals are generally reserved for the high-profile books).

When you are pitching your books yourself, you can target both the bigger and smaller/medium houses, although it's a good idea to bring in an agent to handle negotiations with the larger houses. Alternatively, try contacting the smaller and mid-sized publishers yourself, while looking for an agent to contact the larger publishers, since some agents prefer to contact these publishers themselves and don't want to take on a book that has been shopped around. On the other hand, many agents may be glad to step in once you have contacted publishers and gotten an initial expression of interest. The policies and personal preferences of agents vary widely. In any case, making the initial contacts yourself can speed up the process, since it sometimes takes several months or more to get an agent. But once you have generated some publishing interest, so the agent just has to follow-up, the agent may be ready to come aboard right away.

Deciding Who to Contact

Once you have assessed your manuscript and have decided what types of publishers and editors to target, the next step is determining who to contact. You need a current list, since there is a great deal of change in the publishing industry—especially in the larger houses. For the most part, the smaller houses don't have such a high rate of change, since they are often small partnerships and family affairs, with a publisher and a few editors who are there year after year. But the larger publishers have a lot of turn-over, especially at the assistant to senior editor level. And in recent years, this pace of turnover has increased even more due to all the mergers, acquisitions, and downsizing.

Once you do have current data, direct your query to a specific editor, since a general query, such as one directed to "the editor", will usually get deleted or tossed as junk mail or put at the bottom of an unsolicited queries file. While you can find assorted sources of information online or in the library at no charge, often these listings are incomplete, outdated, or provide only general information, such as the publishers name, address, and phone number. But they don't provide detailed information on specific names of editors or what they or their publishing house are most interested in publishing. Also, while many popular guides to editors and publishers might be a good source of general information (such as *Writer's Market* and the *Writer's Guide to Book Editors, Publishers, and Agents*), these guides are often outdated when it comes to the listings for specific editors (particularly the new ones who are the most likely to be gone). These guides also won't have the latest e-mails or addresses for editors and publishers who have recently moved. The big problem in using these guides is the time between when the researcher collected the information and the date when they are published. The result is that, by the time they first appear in bookstores, they are already about 3-4 months behind—and the use of future dates can be misleading, such as when a 2006 guide is actually published in the fall of 2005.

You usually can't get this information by calling yourself, because if you don't know who to contact, you often can't find out when you call, since the receptionists at the big companies will not give out any names. They will only confirm if a person is still there if you have their name. And if you get voice mail, still need the name to check if the editor is still there.

It is also time-consuming to go from Website to Website seeking current information, and many Websites are designed to sell books and don't have editors' names and contact information. Thus, you need a really up-to-date list, such as used by PublishersandAgents.net in sending out e-mail or postal queries.

Sending Your Queries to Editors and Publishers

When you send a query to an editor, you can send it by either e-mail (if available) or by regular mail, though e-mail is more efficient, and about 85% of the editors are now receptive to e-mails. It is generally best not to call first, since most editors will ask you to send a query in writing.

Start with a written query first, and don't include your manuscript initially (except in the case of picture books for children), since almost universally, editors don't want unsolicited manuscripts. If you send an e-mail query, include your contact information at the end, including your e-mail address. For a postal query, include an SASE, so you are more likely to get a reply. If you include a check list for a response, either on a letterhead or postcard, that can speed up and make a reply more likely, too. Usually editors will not ask for an exclusive look, since they expect multiple submissions—unlike agents, who will sometimes ask for a short time to do their review, typically about 2-4 weeks.

Since it is not always certain what editors want, how receptive they are to new projects, and the types of material of current interest, a good way to make a first contact is to send an email with a few paragraphs (all in the body of the email; no attachments!) or send an initial query letter and 1-2 pages of a more detailed description about your project and yourself. Then, if editors are interested, they can ask to see more. This initial query approach is cost-effective, too, besides being preferred by editors, since it cuts down on the expense of sending more detailed full proposals or outlines and chapters on the first round. You are only sending additional materials to editors who request them.

Another advantage of this initial brief approach is you can send out multiple queries quickly and at little expense, since you are sending a short email at virtually no cost—or sending a letter with 2-3 pages of additional information at a cost of about $.75 a query (though add in some extra costs for labor if you hire someone do this for you). This multiple query approach also increases your chances of finding an editor and choosing among those interested in your project, since even with careful targeting, many editors will not respond or be interested for various reasons. For example, my own pitches to editors several times a year have averaged a 25% response rate. About half of those responding have wanted to see a proposal, and about half of those have been interested enough to take the next step—pitching it to other editors, marketing people, or their publisher, and PublishersAndAgents clients generally report similar results. It's an approach that has resulted in the sale of 1-3 books a year, and this is how I have gotten most of my 40+ books published).

So send multiple queries. It ups your chances of finding interested editors, and with multiple editors expressing interest, you increase your chances of not only placing your book, but getting a better deal.

A good way to select and contact editors is with a coded editors/publishers data-base, so you can select the editors and publishers most appropriate for your project. Or use a submission service like PublishersAndAgents to do this selection for you.

In selecting these editors, if you are using emails, you can query multiple editors at the same house or who work for the same division or imprint at the very large publishers, since emails are shorter and more informal. But if multiple editors at the same house or division express interest, it is best to send your proposal or manuscript to only one editor or check with ask the editors whether to send this material to two or more editors. You can follow-up by phone or email to find out which editor to select. Just let the editors who have expressed interest know that you have gotten multiple requests for your material, and ask who you should send it to. In some cases, I have found that one editor prefers to review it; in other cases, the editors have asked me to send it to both, particularly when one works for the other).

If you are sending out your queries by a regular letter, it is best to only send a query to one editor at a particular house at a time—or perhaps two or three if this is a larger publishing house with a dozen or more editors. Then, if one editor doesn't respond in a few weeks, you can query another. Commonly, in the smaller houses, one letter is all you need, since if an editor isn't interested he or she is likely to pass it on to another editor who is, which is how I got several of my books published.

The advantage of e-mail is it is quick, easy, and inexpensive with editors who are receptive to this approach. The editor can simply hit "reply" to respond. But in case the editor downloads your e-mail for a later response or prefers to call you, be sure to include your name, e-mail address, and phone number in the body of your e-mail.

However, a minority of editors still prefer regular mail and some don't want any email queries. So to contact them, use the old-fashioned letter way. And even if regular mail is slower and more expensive, letter queries do look more professional. If you do send your query by regular letter, include an SASE to increase your chances of getting a response. You can use printed labels on your envelopes or run them through your computer to create them more quickly.

Sending More Information to Interested Editors and Publishers

Once an editor or publisher has expressed interest, he or she typically wants to see certain basic materials. While different editors/publishers have slightly different requests for what they want, generally, they want to see the following materials, which are the same as you would send to a prospective or current agent. So when you send of your queries, have these materials prepared and ready to go as soon as you get any requests to send them.

An advantage of creating this basic package is you have the information that most editors will want on hand for a fast reply—and you can add or subtract materials from this basic package depending on the editor's requests. This is the approach I have used in sending proposals to editors, resulting in over 3 dozen sales.

For Nonfiction—Send a proposal package which includes:

> Table of Contents
> Overview of the book
> Chapter by chapter outline, with brief descriptions for each Chapter
> 1-3 sample chapters (50-80 pages)
> Description of the market
> Your bio, including your credentials for writing the book, and
> any promotional support you can provide

For Fiction—Send the following:

> Brief synopsis
> 1-3 sample chapters (20-50 pages)
> Then be ready to send the complete manuscript on request

For Children's Books

> For younger children: send the whole picture book (if you didn't already send it with your query letter).
> For young adult readers: follow the nonfiction or fiction guidelines

WRITING A GOOD SUBJECT LINE

Your subject line is critical. It makes the difference in whether your query will be opened and read. It also affects whether your query arrives, because of spam filters which screen out certain words or word combinations.

Avoid general or vague descriptions or phrases that sound like sales hype, such as "Great New Novel," "Exciting Dramatic Action Screenplay." And unless your title is self-explanatory, don't put it in the subject line, since it will be confusing or meaningless to the recipient. Instead, include the title in the first or second sentence of your body copy, as you explain what your project is about.

The best approach to the subject line is to specifically indicate the type of book or genre of the film you are submitting for consideration and briefly state the main theme or plot. Keep your subject line short—no more than 15-20 words, and avoid words that are commonly identified as spam such as "sexy," "sexual," and "free." You can use either Title case (Words Start with Caps, Unless They Are Short Words like "and" or "the") or Sentence case (First word capitalized, then the rest are lower case) as you prefer.

If you have any major credits or are an agent yourself, then you can mention this in the subject line; otherwise, leave any bio information for the body of the query.

For example:
    "Romantic comedy about a woman searching for love with all the wrong men"
    "Sci-fi drama about humans who live forever by previously produced screenplay writer"
    "Action Adventure Features Ex-Sheriff in Search of Wife's Killer After a Mysterious Explosion"

Here are some examples from books, scripts, and TV projects we have signed as a result of queries:

"Drama/Action Thriller about a Federal prosecutor matching wits with a charming African-American drug dealer"

"TV Reality or Game Show or Documentary Film Based on Popular Web Site and Book."

Think of writing a subject line like writing a headline for an ad and the rest of your letter like a marketing pitch letter. Your subject line is what gets the recipient to open the door. Then, the rest of the letter is like the hallway, where the recipient decides whether to go inside to learn more.

WRITING A GOOD QUERY LETTER TO SELL YOUR SCRIPT OR TV PROJECT

E-mail queries can be an effective way to open the door to sell your script or TV project, since the majority of producers, production companies, agents, and managers now read and respond to e-mail queries. But you have to use the right approach to get through the door.

Writing a Good Subject Line

Your subject line is critical. It will make the difference in whether your query will be opened and read. It can also affect whether your query arrives, because of spam filters which screen out certain words or word combinations.

Avoid general or vague descriptions or phrases that sound like sales hype, such as "Great New Script," "Exciting Dramatic Action Screenplay." And unless your title is self-explanatory, don't put this in the subject line—it's better to include the title in the first or second sentence of your body copy.

Rather, specifically indicate the genre of your film or type of TV project and briefly state the essence of what this is about. Keep your subject line short—no more than 15-20 words, and avoid words that are commonly identified as spam such as "sexy," "sexual," and "free." You can use either Title case (Words Start with Caps, Unless They Are Short Words like "and" or "the") or Sentence case (First word is capitalized, then the rest are in lower case) as you prefer.

If you have any major credits or are an agent, you can mention this in the subject line; otherwise, leave any bio information for the body of the query.

For example:

"Action Adventure Features Ex-Sheriff in Search of Wife's Killer After a Mysterious Explosion"

"Romantic comedy about a woman searching for love with all the wrong men"

"Sci-fi drama about humans who live forever by previously produced screenplay writer"

Here are some examples from scripts and TV projects we have signed as a result of queries: "Drama/Action Thriller about a Federal prosecutor matching wits with a charming African-American con artist" "Reality or Game Show Based on Popular Web Site and Book ..."

Think of writing a subject line like writing a headline for an ad and the rest of your letter like a marketing pitch letter. Your subject line is what gets the recipient to open the door. Then, the rest of the letter is like the hallway, where the recipient decides whether to go inside to learn more.

Writing a Good Query Letter

Now that you've got the film industry professional's attention, here's what to do in the rest of your letter.

Keep your query short and to the point—ideally around 250-350 words.

Start off with a short sentence for your log-line. Put the essence of what your script is about here. Think of this opening as the kind of summary statement you might use in a pitch meeting when someone asks what your script is about. You can then add an additional sentence to expand on this, such as pointing up how your script is in the tradition of feature films or TV shows that have done well (ie: a thriller in the spirit of *Flight Plan*; a sci-fi/fantasy film with the appeal of *Lord of the Rings* and *Harry Potter*). Stay away from hyperboles, such as the "greatest," "terrific," or "exciting new," since this will sound like self-serving hype, and it is a turn-off for many people.

Next summarize the highlights of your synopsis in 2-3 paragraphs. Write it so it's a tight, clearly written summary, and only include the names of the main characters and main plot elements. If you try to say too much, it will be hard to follow the story, and the reader can lose interest. The idea is to use the query to get the producer, agent, or manager to want to know more by reading your more detailed synopsis or the full script.

Then, in a sentence or two, mention a little about yourself, particularly if you have had previous credits in the film industry. Previous book credits help, too, especially if your book has done well and your film or TV project is based on your book. If you can help to support and promote the film in any way, mention this, such as being able to come to the area where the film is being shot to help with development.

Put any contact information at the end, rather than on top, as in a regular letter, and preferably address your letter by name to a particular person rather than "To Whom It May Concern," "Dear Director," or the like. If you have a Web site, include this, along with your city, state, phone number and e-mail. Even though the letter will go out under your e-mail, include it in your contact information.

HOW TO GET YOUR COLUMN OR ARTICLE SYNDICATED

Would you like to see an article or column you have written published in more than one publication or magazine? Ideally, find a syndicate which acts like an agent to represent you, which is usually more effective and efficient, since they already have the contents and billing procedures in place, though they take about 40-50%. Or consider self-syndication.

While this can be a way to earn money for each article that is published, many writers seek to syndicate an article or column to promote a book they have written or gain more credibility as an expert in an area. It's also a way to better get a book contract or speak, do workshops and seminars or consult in this area.

A good first step is to get your article or column published someplace, even if you do it for free or for a small amount. This way you gain some visibility and build your credibility, since you now have a published article or column.

Unless you are interested in self-syndication, where you send queries to newspapers, magazines, online outlets, and other publishers and follow-up to make sure you get paid, look for a syndication service—or syndicate—to represent you. While syndicates take 40-50% of your income, it can be worth that payment, since they already have an established reach and reputation. Additionally, with a syndicate representing you, you can focus on writing and promoting your article or column. You don't have to get involved in distribution, too.

This article will focus on using this two-step process of first getting your article or column published and then finding a syndicate to represent you.

Getting Your Column or Article Published

When you syndicate an article or column, don't expect to get what writers often get for sole rights or first rights articles—such as $1-2 a word or more in top markets; 50-75¢ a word in others. More typically, syndicated articles sell for about $15-25 for a 700-1000 word article or even less, with the sale typically based on only first time rights for that particular market.

Alternatively, consider your article or column as mainly a promotional vehicle, where a publication runs your contribution for free in return for including your bio, promotional information, e-mail, and Website (if you have one) at the end of the article. Then, while a syndicate might be possibility, try to get a newswire service, which doesn't pay, to pick it up and send it out to its national media clients.

A way to improve your ability to find a syndicate is to be willing to accept whatever publishing deals you can get, since it is more important to BE PUBLISHED in the beginning, as long as you are published in a fairly reputable publication. You can then use that publication as leverage in finding a syndicate to represent you.

For instance, try your nearest major city newspaper or a local weekly. Focus on getting two publications if you can, and if the first publisher wants to run your article series for free in return for bio information about you, do it. That publication will help you get the next publisher, and perhaps this next publisher will be willing to pay. Once you do find a paying publisher, take into consideration the circulation size of the publication in setting your price, and be willing to negotiate down if necessary, since initially, it is more important to be published.

That's what I did with my column, which was syndicated in a dozen papers, including the <u>Oakland Tribune</u> and <u>L.A. Downtown News</u>, and subsequently turned into a book. When I first approached the <u>Oakland Tribune</u>, the editor told me the publisher usually paid around $65 for an article of the size I was proposing—about 800-900 words. Yet, while the editor loved my column, the publisher turned it down because he didn't want to pay for an outside column. So I offered to do the column in return for a bio of about 50 words, and the editor pitched her publisher again. This time he agreed—and the arrangement was that my column would not only run in the Tribune but in 10 other East Bay papers.

The Trib wanted first rights for this market, but meanwhile, I could pitch the column anywhere else.

Then, with that agreement in place, I proposed the column to the <u>L.A. Downtown News</u>, a daily paper looking for lifestyle and career articles to appeal to about 50,000 business and professional people in the downtown L.A. area. This editor liked my column, too, and after some discussion about the cost of individual columns or a series of 13 of them, we settled on about $20 an article for 13, rather than $35 for just one. (The original price was based on about half of what the Tribune would have paid if it paid anything, since this was a smaller paper, and we worked out a package price for multiple copies). Having this column in turn made it possible me to package these columns and add some additional chapters to create a book which became *A Survival Guide for Working with Humans*, published by AMACO, and that led to a follow-up book: *A Survival Guide for Working with Bad Bosses,* because the first one did so well.

Thus, even if you start with a non-paying column, you can turn this into a well-paying source of income.

Getting Copies of Your Column or Article/Series

Once you have a publisher or two, the next step is using your published article or columns to sell yourself to a syndicate or to other publishers if you go the self-syndication route.

Ideally, unless this is a single reprint article, wait for at least 3 to 4 and preferably 5 columns in one publication. If it's a weekly column or article series, you should have these in about a month.

When these articles appear, clip out copies from the print publication—or download the online copies. Then you can either print them out for sending submissions by regular mail or turn them into PDFs or JPEGs for online submissions.

If you are using clips, paste them up neatly with the masthead or name of the publication and the date. Then, you can make copies with a copy machine, or scan them into a GIF file and open that up in a word processing or publishing program (such as Word or Microsoft Publisher) which you can print out. If you use an online version, download the publication masthead and your article into a word processing or publishing program which you can print out or put into a file of clips and send as an attachment.

Additionally, along with your submission, include a bio sheet, highlighting your expertise in the area which is the subject of your material. If your column or article already ends with a strong bio, or if you have a Web site with extensive material about you, direct the syndicate contact there.

Selecting the Syndicates to Contact

To select a syndicate, contact the medium-sized and larger syndicates that handle submissions from outside writers. There are several hundred syndicates listed in the annual Syndicate Directory published by Editor and Publisher each August. You have to do further research to select receptive syndicates, since these listings don't provide much more than address and contact information, though some of the larger syndicates have ads showing who they represent. You also have to exclude the great many syndicates that are self-syndicators or companies representing just a few writers and not looking to handle others. This process can take some time, but that's what PublishersAndAgents.net does each year in updating its own syndicate database.

The key criteria to consider in choosing a syndicate are:

- <u>Types of columns and articles handled</u>. Ideally, look for a syndicate that already handles your type of column or article series, although a syndicate may not want to handle your material if it's directly competitive with something they already handle.

- <u>Location.</u> Although syndicates are located all over the U.S., the largest ones are in the major cities, including New York, Los Angeles, the San Francisco Bay Area, San Diego, Chicago, and Kansas City. Generally, in selecting syndicates to contact, look for those in the larger cities.

- <u>Size of Syndicate.</u> Ideally, look for a syndicate that has the largest number of subscribers or members, since those are potential buyers for your article or column. Another indicator of the power of a syndicate is the number of writers it represents and the star-power of these writers. Preferably, look for a syndicate which has: 1) the most subscribers or members, 2) the most writer clients, and 3) the most high-profile writers. While it may be more difficult to get the most powerful syndicates to handle your material initially, consider going back later if you have been initially rejected once you have built up more credits, possibly by using a smaller syndicate for the first year or two.

Sending Queries to Syndicates

When you send a query to a syndicate, start with an initial e-mail or postal query letter, unless the syndicate specifically invites you to send materials along with your letter. Most syndicates ask for a query letter first. While a formal letter looks more impressive, most syndicates are now receptive to an initial query by e-mail. Generally, don't send a fax unless you first get permission to do so, and at most, use the phone to check whether there is enough interest in your idea to send an initial query or to check for recent contact changes. Since there are usually only one or a few contacts at any syndicate, it is often faster and easier to send out your initial query by e-mail with a sample at the end of the letter or with a cover letter and a few samples in a postal query.

If you already have an article or column published, you can include a sample at the end of your e-mail or along with your letter. Besides briefly describing your article and column in your query, include a brief bio highlighting your credentials and any media you have already gotten. If you have extensive bio information on a Web site, you can include a referral to the URL. This way, your more powerful Web site can speak for you rather than a simple bio sheet.

Alternatively, if you don't already have any published material, send the best of your unpublished articles, along with a bio to emphasize your credentials and how you can help promote your column (and include any Website links, too).

Once you have a request to send the material, send them according to the editor's preferences. While many publications invite e-mail attachments, others want the material included in an e-mail, and others want copies sent by regular mail. Be prepared to follow-up with these alternative approaches.

An advantage of this two-step approach is it enables you to send out multiple queries quickly and at little expense, since you are either following up by e-mail or sending a letter with 2-10 pages of additional information at a cost of about 50c-$1 a query. This multiple query approach also increases your chances of finding a syndicate and choosing among those interested in your project. With multiple syndicates expressing interest at this early stage, you can be more selective in whom to send additional information.

In selecting these syndicates, it is best to only send a query to one person at a particular syndicate. If there are multiple contacts, pick out the person who handles the type of material you have (ie: news, features). Then, if that person isn't the right contact, he or she is likely to pass it on to another contact at that syndicate.

If you are following up by regular mail, most syndicates ask for an SASE for submissions, so include this as a matter of course. You can use printed labels on your envelopes or run them through your computer to speed up creating them. If you are including materials that increase your postage beyond a single stamp, unless you want them returned, include enough postage for a return letter.

Sending More Information to Interested Syndicates

Once a contact at a syndicate has expressed interest, have your materials ready to send—generally in standard double-spaced format. Include a short bio of about 25-50 words at the end, and include any contact information, including your Web site and e-mail address. Some publications may not use all of your bio or contact information, but usually they will be willing to include at least an e-mail address so that readers can contact you with comments or possible story ideas for future columns or articles.

PART II
GUIDELINES

INTRODUCTION TO THE GUIDELINES SECTION

Following you will see the guidelines suggested for sending query letters to book publishers and agents; film producers, production companies, agents, and managers; and syndicatesa. Most of these guidelines are for writing an e-mail query letter. But the basic query letter can be used for both, with some modifications in formatting. Basically, just eliminate the subject line, put the contact information in your letterhead, and mention any material you are including with the letter, such as a more descriptive outline, overview, and bio material.

The basic structure of the guidelines for different industries is the same.

- Keep it short.

- Begin with a brief summary sentence or logline highlighting what's most important.

- Describe your project in 2-3 more paragraphs, highlighting the major topics or plot elements; avoid talking about your project in generalities or superlatives.

- Include some bio information about yourself and/or your company, highlighting what's most relevant to your project.

- Feature any past media coverage, awards, publications, honors, sales you have gotten.

- Point out how you may be able to help support or promote your project in the future.

- End by asking the contact to let you know if interested and offer to send more information by e-mail or regular mail.

While many people end with a comment like: "thank you for your time and consideration," I tend to think this sounds amateurish, like you are asking the person for favors, rather than submitting a proposal for something that the person will find interesting and valuable.

This section is organized into the following categories; in the next section, there are sample letters for each of these categories.

- Book Publishing

- Syndicating Articles and Columns

- Screenplay Writing

Skip to the guidelines for the type of query you want to send.

BOOK PUBLISHING

<u>Guidelines for an E-Mail Query</u>

Keep your query short and to the point—ideally around 300-400 words, and no more than 500. Fill in the details as indicated, though put the letter in your own words. Also, don't use bold type, underlines, or italics, since it is best to send out your query as a text message, which is most likely to be received and read. Use CAPS for emphasis instead.

In the following template, the CAPS are instructions to fill in with your own information.

Subject Line: (HIGHLIGHT THE MAIN POINT OF YOUR BOOK AND BE SPECIFIC; THIS LINE IS VERY IMPORTANT. IT IS WHAT APPEARS IN THE BROWSER ADDRESS LINE, AND IT IS WHAT WILL GET THE EDITOR, AGENT, PRODUCER, OR OTHER RECIPIENT TO OPEN UP YOUR E-MAIL QUERY)

Dear ************ : (THE EDITOR'S/AGENT'S NAME WILL BE FILLED IN HERE; IT WILL BE FILLED IN AUTOMATICALLY IF YOU USE A MERGE PROGRAM; PUBLISHERS AND AGENTS USES SPECIAL SOFT-WARE TO FILL IN THE PERSON'S NAME FOR EACH QUERY)

Would you be interested in my [NONFICTION BOOK/NOVEL) TITLE which is about (DESCRIBE THE SUBJECT AREA OR PLOT IN 20 WORDS OR LESS).

It features (DESCRIBE THE HIGHLIGHTS OF THE BOOK IN 1-2 PARA-GRAPHS; ABOUT 5-8 SENTENCES; HIGHLIGHT THE MAJOR SUB-JECTS COVERED OR MAJOR PLOT POINTS).

TITLE should be highly marketable in that (GIVE ONE OR MORE REA-SONS, SUCH AS "IT IS THE FIRST BOOK TO COVER THIS TOPIC FROM THIS PERSPECTIVE" AND DESCRIBE HOW YOU WILL HELP TO SUPPORT THE BOOK THROUGH YOUR OWN PROMOTIONAL EFFORTS).

(NOW WRITE A PARAGRAPH ABOUT YOUR EDUCATION, BACK-GROUND, EXPERIENCE, ORGANIZATIONAL MEMBERSHIPS, OR OTHER FACTORS THAT SHOW WHY YOU ARE IN AN IDEAL POSI-TION TO WRITE AND PROMOTE THIS BOOK.)

I would be happy to submit a (OVERVIEW/PROPOSAL/SAMPLE CHAP-TER/COMPLETE NOVEL) or other materials for your further consideration. I can also submit (MENTION ANYTHING THAT MIGHT HELP PRO-MOTE THE BOOK, SUCH AS PROMOTIONAL MATERIALS, LETTERS OF ENDORSEMENT FROM WELL-KNOWN PEOPLE IN THE FIELD, NEWS CLIPS OF PREVIOUS PUBLICITY, A LIST OF THINGS YOU MIGHT DO TO PROMOTE THE BOOK, ETC.)

I hope you will be interested in pursuing (TITLE OF YOUR BOOK), and I look forward to hearing from you.

Sincerely,

YOUR NAME
YOUR ADDRESS
YOUR CITY, STATE, ZIP
YOUR E-MAIL
YOUR PHONE NUMBER

Guidelines for a Postal Query

Ideally keep you cover letter to a single page—about 300-400 words, 500 tops. A good approach is to send a short 200-300 word letter, and include a 2-3 page flyer which includes a brief 1-3 sentence paragraph introducing your book (possibly in larger 13-14 point type) and a short excerpt from your proposal, overview, or first few pages of your novel (generally in regular 12 point type) to provide more detail and an example of your style. Here's a sample guide you can follow.

ON YOUR OWN LETTERHEAD:

YOUR COMPANY NAME
YOUR ADDRESS
YOUR CITY, STATE, ZIP
YOUR PHONE—FAX—E-MAIL—WEBSITE

IN YOUR QUERY LETTER:

Date (TO BE FILLED IN)

(Mr./Ms. Editor'S or Agent's First Name Last Name) (THE EDITOR'S/ AGENT'S NAME AND ADDRESS INFORMATION WILL BE FILLED IN HERE; IT WILL BE FILLED IN AUTOMATICALLY IF YOU USE A MERGE PROGRAM; PUBLISHERS AND AGENTS USES SPECIAL SOFT-WARE TO FILL IN THE PERSON'S NAME FOR EACH QUERY)
TITLE
COMPANY
ADDRESS
CITY, STATE, ZIP

Dear **************: (THIS WILL SIMILARLY BE FILLED IN EITHER MANUALLY, BY A MERGE PROGRAM, OR SPECIAL SOFTWARE)

I would like to introduce my (BOOK PROPOSAL/NOVEL) called TITLE, a (FICTION/NONFICTION) book in the subject area(s) of (LIST SUBJECTS).

(IN THE NEXT 1-2 PARAGRAPHS, PROVIDE A BRIEF OVERVIEW OF MAIN SUBJECTS COVERED IN THE BOOK OR THE MAIN PLOT POINTS, ABOUT 5-8 SENTENCES.)

TITLE should be marketable to a wide audience in that (GIVE ONE OR MORE REASONS, SUCH AS: "IT APPEALS TO A WIDE RANGE OF AGES AND INTERESTS" OR "THIS TOPIC HAS NEVER BEEN COV-ERED FROM THIS PERSPECTIVE" ETC.)

(NOW INCLUDE A PARAGRAPH ABOUT YOUR EDUCATION, BACK-GROUND, EXPERIENCE, AND ANY AWARDS, DISTINCTIONS, OR ORGANIZATION MEMBERSHIPS THAT ARE RELEVANT TO WRITING AND/OR YOUR SUBJECT.)

I would be happy to submit a (PROPOSAL OVERVIEW/SAMPLE CHAPTER) or a (COMPLETE PROPOSAL/COMPLETE NOVEL) for your further consideration. I can also submit (MENTION ANYTHING THAT MAY HELP PROMOTE THE BOOK, SUCH AS PROMOTIONAL MATERIALS, LETTERS OF ENDORSEMENT FROM PEOPLE IN THE FIELD, NEWS CLIPS IF THIS HAS GOTTEN ANY PREVIOUS PUBLICITY, A LIST OF THINGS YOU MIGHT DO TO PROMOTE THE BOOK, ETC.)

I hope you will be interested in pursuing TITLE, and I look forward to hearing from you.

Sincerely,

YOUR NAME

Flyer or Synopsis for a Postal Query

This flyer that goes along with your cover letter is designed to describe your project in more detail. It is a 1-2 page overview or synopsis of your project. The following example is a little long at 3 pages, but it is a fairly complex and dramatic story, and the submission gained the interest of an agent and consideration by some TV producers. It starts off with a brief introduction to the project, followed by the first few pages from the overview to the proposal. I have changed some identifying details for confidentiality.

MY NAME ISN'T JULIA

A Proposed Book and TV Special by Julia Evans with Gini Graham Scott, Ph.D., J.D.

It's a story of a woman, Julia, who escaped from oppression in a Communist country into domestic violence and abuse by a half-brother resulting in a child, a trial, a conviction, and eventual triumph in Canada, her adopted country. The escape from Yugoslavia to the United States is like a filmed adventure story, with a six week trek through the mountains, a run from the police and their dogs, a day hiding in the river and losing food supplies, and a voyage to the United States in a container for machinery on a ship, before being discovered by sailors and turned over to immigration. Meanwhile, once on the ship, the violence and abuse started, escalating from occasional beatings to being kept hostage, suffering from regular violence and sexual abuse, and having a child. Finally, after a day of being tied to a chair and beaten, Julia made her dramatic escape to her apartment manager's office, followed by the arrest of her half-brother, and his trial, conviction, and 7 year sentence—all covered by the media. Now, after two years in a safe house and recovery from the trauma, the woman, now living with a boyfriend and working in his store as they raise her child, tells her story.

From the Introduction to the Proposal

My story reads like the plot of a movie thriller, featuring a daring escape from poverty in an oppressive communist country only to be held hostage and subject to violence and abuse by my increasingly paranoid and mentally disturbed half-brother, who helped me escape. But soon he began raping and beating me, and I had his child. I was too afraid to escape because he threatened to kill me and my child and I knew little English. Finally, after three years, when I saw my chance, I did break away, leading to his arrest, followed by a headline making trial, resulting in his conviction and 7 year sentence, to be followed by deportation. Soon after that, I won my battle to stay in my adopted country, Canada, and found a job, a supportive boyfriend, and a mission to help other women who have suffered abuse.

This story is not a screen role or script I wanted to play. Yet, now that it has happened and I have come to terms with the trauma, I feel recovered physically and psychologically and am ready to tell my story.

It began in a village in Yugoslavia. I grew up in a poor family, with an older brother, and four younger brothers and sisters. My father had been a policeman, while my mother never worked, and we lived on his small pension. We ate mostly vegetables and could only afford shoes once a year, because we were so poor.

I briefly met my half-brother Simon in 1987 when I was 16 and he was 30. He was on a weekend vacation from attending school in another town, and he had just been released from prison for physical assault, robbery, and rape charges. His imprisonment was his latest brush with the law after a troubled past dating from when he was put in an orphanage after his father married my mother. As a teenager, he became an army deserter and spent the next years in and out of prison. At the time I met Simon, my parents warned me about telling him where I was going to school, although he treated me very nicely, like I was a little sister.

That's why I trusted Simon when I saw him 7 years later in 1995, when I was 24 and living in my own apartment. I was struggling desperately to survive, working full time in a restaurant seven days a week on a low salary that only covered the rent, plus I got meals when I worked.

When Simon stopped by to visit me after his latest release from prison, I told him how much I wanted to get away because things were so difficult, and he suggested going to the United States. At once I wanted to go, and besides finding a better life for myself, I hoped to send money to help my parents. Since we needed money to get there, I borrowed money from my cousin, and we left at the end of August, 1995.

While much of the trip through Yugoslavia to the border was routine, after that everything became like an adventure film that spun rapidly out of control. Simon and I couldn't simply take the train to Europe, since we had no documents to get out of Yugoslavia. So we hiked through the mountains to get to Italy. Along the way, we had to avoid the police, since Simon said he had committed a crime there and could be arrested if we were discovered. As a result, we lost all of our food and clothing one day, when we had to jump into the river to avoid the police. Finally, after a month of walking and living off the land, we arrived in Italy, where we briefly stayed in a shelter, and eventually we got to Genoa, where we slept in the forest for several days.

But just when I thought everything would be fine, since I could find work to earn money for our journey to the United States, everything changed. Instead of being my protector, Simon told me I couldn't leave him, threatened to kill me, hit me, and said he would only let me go free after we got to the United States. I was too scared to resist, and I didn't know any Italian, though Simon did. So over the next weeks, I stayed with him in Italy and did what he wanted. Instead of going to work, I helped him steal food and other goods, which he sold in Genoa and

Venice. Though Simon often beat me, hitting me in the face or head with his fist, I felt helpless to resist.

Then, in February, 1996, when we found a ship going to the United States and stowed away by hiding in a large container, after several near brushes with the police, things got even worse. We were in the container with another Yugoslavian man, and Simon said I needed to show the man I was his wife, so he insisted we had to have sex. Otherwise, he threatened to kill me and put the pieces in the garbage bags in the container which we used to relieve ourselves. This was the beginning of his regular sexual assaults, sometimes every day or every other day.

When we arrived in Idaho after 2 weeks, Simon said I had to tell the U.S. government we were married, though he reassured me he would free me after a month or two once we got the documents to stay in the U.S. But the situation got worse as he continued to beat me and abuse me sexually. We briefly stayed at the YMCA for a month, where I started to learn some Spanish, and we moved to an apartment in March. I had to stay home cooking and cleaning, while Simon went out to look through garbage cans for food, liquor, and clothing, and his threats to kill me if I tried to leave kept me there. He also continued to beat me, though not on the head and face, so when we went out for occasional walks and met other Yugoslavians, no one would suspect anything. Meanwhile, his sexual demands became even more brutal, especially when he used a large vibrator, and he became increasingly paranoid. He heard voices calling my name and he began sleeping with a knife under the bed, so he could threaten me or any strangers coming to get me, although when he got up to search the balcony for intruders, no one was ever there.

I felt like killing myself because the situation seemed so hopeless, but I couldn't do it, and in September I got pregnant. Though I wanted an abortion, Simon refused, saying if we had a child, it would be easier to get the documents to stay in the U.S. He claimed I would end up in jail if I tried to get an abortion and the true story of our illegal entry into the U.S. got out. So I felt I had to go along with what he wanted. At least the beatings stopped while I was pregnant, though Simon continued to insist on having sex each day. Occasionally, we would go out with another Yugoslavian couple, but it was impossible to tell them anything. Also, Simon was so jealous, that if another man even looked at me, as happened when we traveled from Idaho to Oregon with another couple, he would beat me again.

Then, in June 1997, I had my baby, who despite everything, was born healthy and normal. After that, I continued to live in a kind of prison for almost a year, with Simon as my paranoid jailer. The beatings and brutal sex continued, and Simon even got a tape recorder which he left with me when he left the apartment, so he could make sure I was always there and could tell if anyone came into the apartment when he was away. His threats to kill me also became more frequent, and he even spoke of taking our baby to Italy to sell him.

My chance to escape came when Simon became very suspicious and violent, because he suspected me of having sex with a former apartment manager. He suspected this after he found a note with an address in the apartment which he thought might be the manager's. He tied me up in a chair for about 12 hours and questioned me like I was a condemned prisoner making my last confession. Again and again, he hit me with a bat, piece of wood, and belt buckle, and gagged me with an old rag. Finally, he agreed to let me live if I would go to the man he thought was my lover and tell him it was all over between us and record it on a cassette tape. But since I didn't know the former manager's address, I told him I would ask the new manager for it, and that's when I had a chance to escape. I told the manager to call the police, and after they arrived, I told them how Simon had tied me up and beaten me the previous day, and spoke about my previous months of abuse. The police arrested him, and soon after that, I went to the first of two safe houses, where I stayed for the next year.

This arrest led to Simon's trial and conviction, and the whole story came out and made headlines. After that, I was finally free, although it has taken me a long time to heal physically and emotionally. I had many sessions with therapists and in group sessions when I was staying in the safe houses, which helped me come to terms with what happened. Learning to accept and move on has been especially hard for me, because besides the beatings and sex abuse, I have had to deal with having sex and a child with my half-brother, which is considered a sin in my religion and very shameful in my culture. Yet, loving my child has helped. Also, I have gained much support in my adopted country, as I have found work in a restaurant, developed a wonderful relationship with my boyfriend, Alex, who I met through a friend at the restaurant. And now I live with Alex, work in his furniture shop, and have gained a circle of supportive friends and neighbors.

Thus, at last I am ready to tell my story, which is described in this book.

SYNDICATING ARTICLES AND COLUMNS

Guidelines for an E-Mail Query

Keep your query short and to the point—ideally around 300-400 words, and no more than 500. Fill in the details as indicated, though put the letter in your own words. Also, don't use bold type, underlines, or italics, since your query will go out as a text message, which is most likely to be received and read. Use CAPS for emphasis instead.

Subject Line: (HIGHLIGHT THE MAIN POINT OF YOUR ARTICLE OR COLUMN. THIS LINE IS VERY IMPORTANT, SINCE THIS IS WHAT GETS THE EDITOR TO OPEN YOUR E-MAIL)

Dear **************: (THE EDITOR'S/DIRECTOR'S NAME WILL BE FILLED IN HERE; IT WILL BE FILLED IN AUTOMATICALLY IF YOU USE A MERGE PROGRAM; PUBLISHERS AND AGENTS USES SPECIAL SOFTWARE TO FILL IN THE PERSON'S NAME FOR EACH QUERY)

I would like to introduce my (ARTICLE/COLUMN) which is about (DESCRIBE THE SUBJECT AREA OR PLOT IN 20 WORDS OR LESS AND NOTE THE TITLE, THEME, OR ANYTHING DISTINCTIVE ABOUT YOUR APPROACH. THEN ADD ANOTHER SENTENCE OR TWO HIGHLIGHT THE MAIN POINTS OF YOUR ARTICLE OR TYPICAL TOPICS COVERED IN YOUR COLUMN. IF YOUR ARTICLE HAS ALREADY BEEN PUBLISHED ANYWHERE, NOTE THIS HERE).

(NOW WRITE A PARAGRAPH ABOUT YOUR CREDENTIALS, EXPERIENCE, AND PROMOTIONAL SUPPORT YOU CAN PROVIDE, SUCH AS SPEAKING, TV/RADIO APPEARANCES, NEWSPAPER INTERVIEWS,

WEB SITE PROMOTION, ETC. HIGHLIGHT WHAT YOU HAVE DONE, AND NOTE WHAT YOU WILL DO IN THE FUTURE).

I would be happy to submit (NUMBER OF COLUMNS YOU HAVE WRITTEN; INVITE THE EDITOR TO INDICATE HOW MANY TO SEND AND IN WHAT FORM—MAIL OR E-MAIL) for your further consideration. I can also submit (MENTION ANYTHING THAT MIGHT HELP PROMOTE YOU AS AN AUTHORITY TO SUPPORT THE ARTICLE OR COLUMN, SUCH AS PROMOTIONAL MATERIALS, LETTERS OF ENDORSEMENT FROM PEOPLE IN THE FIELD, NEWS CLIPS OF PREVIOUS PUBLICITY, A LIST OF THINGS YOU MIGHT DO TO PROMOTE THE BOOK, ETC.)

I hope you will be interested in pursuing (TITLE OF YOUR ARTICLE OR COLUMN), and I look forward to hearing from you.

Sincerely,

YOUR NAME
YOUR ADDRESS
YOUR CITY, STATE, ZIP CODE
YOUR EMAIL
YOUR PHONE NUMBER

Here's a sample of a letter I used in selling my own column.

SUBJECT LINE: Column on Improving Relationships in Work and Business Based on Best-Selling Book by Nationally-Known Author

Would you be interested in publishing or syndicating my weekly column WORK IT RIGHT? on improving relationships in work and business nationally and internationally? It begins with a story or problem, then suggests what the person could do to resolve that problem, should have done, or might do differently in the future. The column has already been picked up by a dozen papers in the San Francisco Bay Area, including the Oakland Tribune. Now I am seeking to expand to other newspapers.

I can help support the column with additional promotional assistance. I have published over 35 books on various topics, including personal development, business, work, lifestyles, pop culture, and social trends. My books have been published by major publishers including Prentice-Hall/Simon & Schuster, Contemporary Books, Pearson, Warner, and Kensington.

I am a speaker, workshop/seminar leader, and consultant on the topics featured in this column, and have been a guest on hundreds of TV and radio shows, including Oprah, Montel Williams, the O'Reilly Factor, CCN News, and other programs. You can see extensive bio and promotional information about me at my Web site at www.giniscott.com, plus copies of articles, columns, and other clips at www.giniscott.net.

I can send you 3-8 samples of my columns by mail or e-mail attachments.

I'll look forward to hearing from you and discussing this column further.

Sincerely,

Gini Graham Scott, Ph.D.
Director, Creative Communications & Research
6114 La Salle, #358
Oakland, CA 94611
CreComRes@aol.com
(510) 339-1625

Guidelines for a Postal Query to Syndicates

Ideally, keep you cover letter to a single page—about 200-300 words. If you have a single article, include that. Or if you are pitching a series of columns, a good approach is to include a one page flyer describing your column or few samples of your column along with your cover letter. Here's a sample guide you can follow.

YOUR COMPANY NAME
YOUR ADDRESS
YOUR CITY, STATE, ZIP
YOUR PHONE—FAX—E-MAIL—WEBSITE

Date

EDITOR'S OR AGENT'S NAME (MR./MS. FIRST NAME LAST NAME)
TITLE, IF ANY
COMPANY
ADDRESS
CITY, STATE, ZIP

Dear **************:

I would like to tell you about my (ARTICLE/COLUMN) which is about (DESCRIBE THE SUBJECT AREA OR PLOT IN 20 WORDS OR LESS AND NOTE THE TITLE, THEME, OR ANYTHING DISTINCTIVE ABOUT YOUR APPROACH. ADD A SENTENCE OR TWO TO HIGH-LIGHT THE MAIN POINTS OF YOUR ARTICLE OR REPRESENTA-TIVE SUBJECTS COVERED IN YOUR COLUMNS. IF YOUR ARTICLE HAS ALREADY BEEN PUBLISHED ANYWHERE, NOTE THIS HERE).

(NOW WRITE A PARAGRAPH ABOUT YOUR CREDENTIALS, EXPERI-ENCE, AND PROMOTIONAL SUPPORT YOU CAN PROVIDE, SUCH AS SPEAKING, TV/RADIO APPEARANCES, NEWSPAPER INTERVIEWS, WEB SITE PROMOTION, ETC. HIGHLIGHT WHAT YOU HAVE DONE AND WILL DO IN THE FUTURE).

I am enclosing (ENCLOSE 1-3 COLUMNS) and would be happy to submit (NOTE THE ADDITIONAL NUMBER OF COLUMNS AVAILABLE; INVITE THE EDITOR TO INDICATE HOW MANY TO SEND AND IN WHAT FORM—E-MAIL OR REGULAR MAIL) for your further consider-ation. I can also submit (MENTION ANYTHING THAT MIGHT HELP PROMOTE YOU AS AN AUTHORITY TO SUPPORT THE ARTICLE OR COLUMN, SUCH AS PROMOTIONAL MATERIALS, LETTERS OF ENDORSEMENT FROM WELL-KNOWN PEOPLE IN THE FIELD, NEWS CLIPS OF PREVIOUS PUBLICITY, A LIST OF THINGS YOU MIGHT DO TO PROMOTE THE BOOK, ETC.)

I hope you will be interested in pursuing (TITLE OF YOUR ARTICLE OR COLUMN), and I look forward to hearing from you. I am enclosing an SASE for your convenience if you want to reply by mail.

Sincerely,

YOUR NAME
TITLE IN COMPANY, IF ANY

Here's a sample of a letter which I sent by postal mail about my own columns.

Creative Communications & Research

6114 La Salle Avenue, #358. Oakland, CA 94611
(510) 339-1625. FAX: 339-1626. CreComRes@aol.com

July 18, 2001

Would you be interested in syndicating my column on improving relationships in work and business nationally and internationally? It begins with a story or problem, then suggests what the person should do, could have done, or should do in the future. The column has already been picked up by a dozen papers—11 in the San Francisco Bay Area, including the Oakland Tribune, and the Los Angeles Downtown News. Now I am looking for a syndication service to take over syndication.

I can help support the column with additional promotional assistance. I have published over 35 books on various topics, including personal development, business, work, lifestyles, pop culture, and social trends. My books have been published by major publishers including Prentice-Hall/Simon & Schuster, Contemporary Books, Pearson, Warner, and Kensington. I am a speaker, workshop/ seminar leader, and consultant on the topics featured in this column, and have been a guest on hundreds of TV and radio shows, including Oprah, Montel Williams, the O'Reilly Factor, CCN News, and other programs. You can see extensive bio and promotional information about me at my Web site at www.giniscott.com, plus copies of articles, columns, and other clips at www.giniscott.net.

I am enclosing samples of the first columns which have appeared in the Oakland Tribune and Los Angeles Downtown News for your review. I have already written 8 columns, and can send you the manuscripts by mail or e-mail attachments.

I'll look forward to hearing from you and discussing your syndication arrangements further.

Sincerely,

Gini Graham Scott, Ph.D.
Director

SCREENPLAY WRITING

<u>Guidelines for Writing an E-Mail Query</u>

Start with a compelling subject line and keep your query short and to the point—ideally around 300-400 words. Begin with a logline of about 25-30 words, followed by a few sentences or paragraph or two about the plot of your script, and include a brief introduction to yourself, emphasizing any credentials that are most relevant to your script. Fill in the details as indicated, though use your own words. Keep everything simple and flush left, so you can send the query in a simple text format that can be read in any e-mail program. Since a text message doesn't have bold type, underlines, or italics, use CAPS instead for emphasis.

Subject Line: (HIGHLIGHT THE MAIN GENRE AND SELLING POINT OF YOUR SCRIPT HERE; THIS IS VERY IMPORTANT, SINCE THIS IS WHAT WILL GET THE CONTACT TO OPEN THE E-MAIL).

Dear ***************: (THE PRODUCER/AGENT'S NAME WILL BE FILLED IN HERE; IT WILL BE FILLED IN AUTOMATICALLY IF YOU USE A MERGE PROGRAM; PUBLISHERS AND AGENTS USES SPECIAL SOFTWARE TO FILL IN THE PERSON'S NAME FOR EACH QUERY):

(SCREENPLAY TITLE) is about (INCLUDE A SHORT 1-SENTENCE LOGLINE HERE; IDEALLY UP TO 25 WORDS.

THEN IN A FEW SENTENCES OR A PARAGRAPH OR TWO DESCRIBE THE MAJOR PLOT POINTS OF THE SCRIPT.

(NOW WRITE A PARAGRAPH ABOUT YOUR CREDENTIALS AND EXPERIENCE, HIGHLIGHTING ANY CREDITS IN THE FILM INDUS-TRY OR EXPERIENCE THAT BEARS DIRECTLY ON THE SUBJECT OF YOUR SCRIPT. NOTE IF YOU ARE ABLE TO COME TO THE AREA WHERE THE PRODUCER IS BASED FOR FURTHER DEVELOPMENT,

AND IF YOU HAVE ANY SPECIAL ABILITY TO RAISE FUNDS, NOTE THIS HERE.)

I would be happy to submit a more detailed synopsis or copy of my script by e-mail or regular mail and look forward to hearing from you.

Sincerely,

YOUR NAME
YOUR ADDRESS
YOUR EMAIL
YOUR PHONE NUMBER

Here's a sample of a letter I might send, using a logline from one of my scripts that was optioned by a producer and is supposed to go into production in 2006.

SUBJECT LINE: Introducing RICH AND DEAD: a cop/action/mystery thriller; based on a true story.

Here's a new script for your consideration—RICH AND DEAD. After a homicide secretary's wealthy friend, seeking divorce, becomes ill, the secretary suspects the husband of poisoning her—and he is.

After her friend's death, with help from her boyfriend and homicide detective, she prevents a cremation and foils efforts to dispose of the body, leading to a chase through an abandoned shipyard and capture of two gunman and the husband.

I have written a dozen scripts, one which is going into production next year with an independent film company, and have published over 35 books with major publishers.

In writing RICH AND DEAD, I have drawn on my experience in working with the Oakland police for five years, and I could assist in making arrangements to obtain the help of the police, other city officials, and the Oakland film commission if the film is shot in Oakland. I spent a year doing a report on homicide patterns for the Oakland Police Department and received a Certificate in the

Administration of Justice from Merritt College in Oakland. I have also received national media exposure for my books, including an appearance on Oprah.

I would be glad to come to Los Angeles to assist with further development. I can send you a copy of the synopsis or the full script in an e-mail attachment in Word, text, or Scriptware or by regular mail. I'll look forward to hearing from you and discussing this project further.

Sincerely,

Gini Graham Scott, Ph.D.
Director, Creative Communications & Research
6114 La Salle, #358
Oakland, CA 94611
(510) 339-1625
CreComRes@aol.com
www.screenworksusa.com

PART III
SAMPLE LETTERS

INTRODUCTION TO THE SAMPLE LETTERS SECTION

The following section features some sample letters which I have written for clients. They are organized according to the type of letter—nonfiction and fiction books, children's books, screenplays, and finally columns. I have changed the identifying data, including the title of the manuscript and some subject matter or plot points, in each letter to protect the identity of the client. So you won't find any of the names and credits mentioned, if you try to research them.

As you'll see the following letters are about 300-500 words and start with the type of project or genre clearly indicated, followed by a brief description of what the book, script, or column is about. Then, the next 2 or 3 paragraphs quickly summarize the main topic or plot, using a narrative or bullet-points. After that, there's a brief introduction to the author—and had he any credits in the subject of the book, script, or column, or in the publishing or film industry. Then, any publications or press are cited, followed by an offer to send material if interest.

All of these letters can be easily formatted as a postal query by just taking off the subject line; putting the letter on a letterhead; adding the usual date, contact name and address, and salutation; and eliminating the contact information at the end, since this is what goes in the letterhead.

SAMPLE LETTERS FOR BOOKS—NONFICTION

Subject Line: Memoir by Katrina Victim Organizing Other Victims to Gain Extra Insurance Coverage; Subject of Extensive Media Coverage

Dear **********:

I am one of the thousands of Katrina victims, and I have a unique story to tell, in that I have used this tragedy to help victims nationally gain extra insurance coverage, which has been gaining extensive media attention. SURVIVING THE STORM tells my story—both what happened during the five days I was trapped in a hospital in New Orleans and about my later efforts to pass the bill for special insurance coverage to help the victims of future hurricanes.

In brief, here's my story. My father died in the Earnest N. Morial Convention Center on September 1, after being evacuated there. Meanwhile, I was unable to go to his aid, since I couldn't leave the city because I, along with my daughter and husband were trapped inside a hospital. Little did we know that from Sunday evening until Friday afternoon when we were airlifted out we would be trapped due to flood water. The experience I encountered will be one that I will never forget. Medical personnel ran around in the dark with tiny flashlights trying to save lives and put in IV's in pitch darkness. Over six hundred people including staff and family members had come to the hospital for shelter. Within one day food was short, and we had a half sandwich and teacup of soup. The smell was deadly. Urine and feces were put in many large hazardous waste bins and there was no water, aside from other things.

Afterwards, it took nearly six weeks to get the remains back of my father so we could give him a proper burial, and we only got her back after my 5 year old daughter and I protested outside of the morgue. I only did so after repeated delays at the hospital and writing to the White House and many other officials.

Now I am working on trying to get a bill passed that would provide additional insurance to those who are not able to afford the insurance necessary to recover after a disaster. To this end, I have been writing and seeking to meet with elected officials in Louisiana, including the Governor, and hope to expand this campaign to other states. These efforts have gained the attention of news reporters from around the world, including the New York Times and L.A. Times, and there are also numerous pictures about my struggle on the Internet.

SURVIVNG THE STORM details what happened to me in the wake of Katrina and how it has affected my life, particularly since I have been devoting every waking moment for the last two months to getting these bills passed.

If you're interested, I can send you a copy of the proposal and sample chapters by e-mail or regular mail, and I look forward to hearing from you.

Sincerely,

Subject Line: Book on Saving the World Due to the Energy Crisis After Fuel Runs Out

Dear **********

THE LAST ENERGY CRISIS ... AND WHAT TO DO ABOUT IT describes how the world is in a crisis since oil and other fuels are running out, leading to a collapse of the world economy if something isn't done soon. This book provides a solution to save the world.

This 40,000 word book describes the current sad state of affairs due to the past 150 years of industrialization fueled by the energy of fossil fuels. But now the fuel is running out and becoming more and more expensive. And in a few years, there won't be enough.

The solution is a new form of energy in the earth, which has been largely unknown until now. The book explains how this source can be tapped.

More specifically, the book includes chapters on these topics:

- Why the world needs saving

- Different forms of energy

- The untapped power of the earth

- How to get this geothermal energy now

- What the world will be like tomorrow after this new source of energy is tapped

The book is designed for a general audience to raise the consciousness of the world, not just a highly technical book no one reads. The book has the appeal of classical environmental works like Rachel's Carson's SILENT SPRING. And it should have broad appeal as the only book on this subject.

I have excellent credentials for writing and promoting this book. I am a nuclear physicist, and I did scientific research in a number of disciplines, including (SPE-CIFIC CREDENTIALS ARE INCLUDED HERE). I am also active in my local community in dealing with environmental issues, and plan to present this book at upcoming conferences in the field and seek endorsements for later editions.

I also expect to be involved in an extensive book promotion, once the book is published. Beyond being available for a national and international book tour, I will develop a Website for the book, which will include the latest developments in dealing with the fuel crisis and developing this new source of energy. In addition, I plan to participate in Earth Day and other environmental events and write articles based on the book to help promote it.

If you're interested, I can send you the book proposal, some sample chapters or the complete manuscript by e-mail or regular mail. I look forward to hearing from you and discussing this book further.

Sincerely,

SAMPLE LETTERS FOR
BOOKS—FICTION

Timely Contemporary Drama About Trafficking in Drugs and Illegal Aliens, a Kidnapping, and a Bomb Plot Along the U.S.-Mexican Border

Dear *********:

BORDER PLOT is about two men who repeatedly delve into illegal activities on the California-Mexican border and repeatedly blow it—from trafficking in drugs and illegal aliens to kidnapping a popular rock star. Meanwhile, their efforts are complicated when three terrorists attempt to blow up the football stadium in L.A. during a game. It is a story that combines serious events with the comedy of two bumbling would-be crooks.

The lead characters are Dan Williams, the organizer of these illegal activities, and John Franklin, his constant follower and supporter, until he turns on Dan in the end. For one of his most thought-out schemes, Dan arranges with a local garage to modify an old van to transfer illegal aliens from McAllen to San Diego. Though he hopes to make a fortune on the deal, the van meets with a tragic accident killing most of the passengers on the way to San Diego. Dan and John both escape being implicated because the van is completely destroyed, and there is no paper trail.

Then, Dan invents a unique method of kidnapping the rock star at a concert in San Bernardino. The kidnapping plot is successful right up until the time a one million dollar ransom is delivered. However, arrangements are complicated when three terrorists attempt to launch a deadly bomb into the L.A. stadium during a football game.

Still, Dan goes ahead with the plan and travels to a small town near Irvine to collect the one million ransom, only to be turned in by his one-time faithful supporter, John, who reports Dan to the authorities. So John gains the ransom money instead, as the final scene of the script reveals. It takes place in the home of John's brother in Mexico, where they are celebrating the one million ransom and John's arrival.

The script should have broad appeal, since it reflects current events along the California-Mexico border that are in the daily news, such as drug smuggling, illegal alien activities, and terrorism.

It's an area I know well, since I have been living in the San Diego area for over 20 years. Besides being active as an investment banker and writing articles on trade with Mexico, I have been a popular speaker for numerous organizations in California. The script is based on a book I self-published and distributed in a limited edition, but plan to distribute more widely when the movie is released.

If you are interested, I can send you a more detailed synopsis or copy of the script by e-mail or regular mail.

Sincerely,

Subject Line: Romance novel of action, passion, peril, and some magic about a woman seeking to regain her castle from her traitorous half-brother and the rival prince she comes to love

Dear *********:

I'm seeking representation for my 90,000 word action packed romance JOURNEY TO THE CASTLE, a story about a 13th century noblewoman, who has special healing powers.

The manuscript would be ideal for publishers who feature historical romances with a light paranormal element, such as Harlequin, Avon Harper Collins, or Berkley. It also has strong film potential at a time when interest in historical and fantasy features is high. Here's a brief overview of the plot:

Judith is a headstrong noblewoman who has special healing powers, but does not use magic to harm others. She leaves the castle to see her father off on crusade, and within hours of their departure, she learns her castle has fallen under siege by her traitorous half brother. The king orders Sir Anthony, a landless dashing knight from a rival house to escort her to safety and lead an army to retake her castle. She isn't happy with this forced allegiance, but has to accept this protectorship and learn to trust Sir Anthony, her only ally, though he's from a family who's been at war with hers for generations.

Sir Anthony, a second son, a master horseman who is determined to do whatever it takes to rise in royal rank, is motivated by the king's secret offering of a reward——her land——if he can conquer the villain-brother who stole her castle. However, on their way to join his army and prepare to battle for her castle, they are ambushed en route by her brother's henchmen and during the fight, Judith discovers she has magical powers, not just healing powers, so she can command a horse to do her will with the power of her mind. As a result, she and Robert are able to escape, and they take shelter in an abandoned manor house, where they let down their guard against each other and fall in love. But then when Judith learns that Sir Anthony has been seeking to win her land, her heart is torn by duty and desire. Meanwhile, Sir Anthony is struggling with his desire to win her land and his love of Judith.

Ultimately, she is captured by her brother and Sir Anthony is determined to win her freedom, despite the risks. And eventually, Judith is able to use her magic to cause her brother's cavalry horses to fall, which turns the tide of the battle. So in the end she wins the knight she loves, destroys her evil half-brother, and saves her castle.

I'm a member of the Romance Writers Association, and JOURNEY TO THE CASTLE has won many awards for unpublished authors. I'm a longtime fan of historical romance, and have extensively researched the history of this period to write this manuscript.

I would be glad to send you a more detailed synopsis, some sample chapters, or the full manuscript on request, and I look forward to hearing from you.

Sincerely,

SAMPLE LETTERS FOR CHILDREN'S BOOKS: PICTURE BOOK

Subject Line: Inspirational Picture Book Tells the Story of How a Monkey Gets a New Name from His Friends Because of the Way He Helps Others

Dear **********

HAPPY HORATIO is a 1000-word picture book about a monkey named HORATIO who helps out his friends in the zoo and gets a new name from them—"Happy Horatio" as a result of his efforts.

Horatio earns his new name in this way;

- First, Horatio helps his friend Ollie the Ostrich overcome his difficulty in reading, so he can read a new book. He finds Oscar the Owl, the smartest animal in the zoo to help him.

- Next, he helps Trixie the Tiger overcome his fear of swimming with the help of Anthony the Otter, the best swimmer in the forest.

- After he his hit in the head with a ball by Henry the Hippo and Georgie the Grizzley Bear who are practicing for a soccer game, he encourages them in kicking ability.

- Then, he sees Peter the Penguin who is swimming laps to be in better shape for the game, he encourages his efforts to be the best he can be.

- Finally, the animals give him his new name because of his help, encouragement, and positive attitude.

The book is designed to show children the power of a positive attitude and out-look on life and never giving up. It is designed to appeal to the growing market for positive, inspirational books for children.

I got the idea for the book as a result of teaching my three-year old daughter and being a counselor for 10 years at a children's summer camp which uses sports to promote a positive attitude.

I would be glad to send you a copy of the full manuscript by e-mail or regular mail, and look forward to hearing from you.

Sincerely,

SAMPLE LETTERS FOR CHILDREN'S BOOKS: YOUNG ADULT BOOK

Subject Line: YA Fantasy Adventure about a girl and his talking cat partner and their on-going struggle to right magic that has gone wrong.

Dear ***********

SAVING THE ELF KING is a 50,000-word book in the tradition of Lord of the Rings, Eragon, and the Harry Potter series, and it similarly has strong movie potential. This book chronicles the adventures of a 13 year-old girl, Anita and her talking cat partner Melinda, who was once a witch. Together they work for the Counter Spells Department of a Magical Protection Agency, in a world where magic and technology are intertwined. It's their job to right magic that has gone wrong, using all of their skills, knowledge and Anita's trusty magical backpack. The website is at ****

In this first book, Anita and Melinda tackle a series of adventures, which include:

• rousting some pesky little red mice that are terrorizing a local residence

• foiling a big dragon's assault on the city

• saving an elf king who is slowly disappearing after drinking a mystical afternoon tea.

Their efforts to save the elf-king turns into a quest to recover a missing ingredient for a potion that takes them to forbidden lands where they encounter magical beasts and unique challenges destined to test all their skills and intelligence. As they travel through the immense woods and deadly swamp, they are able to prevail with the help of a brave elf ranger and Anita's magical backpack. Though now they meet an even greater challenge when they encounter devious pirates at sea, they are able to prevail with the help of a friendly whale, and eventually they must recover a talisman from the lair of a very large and ferocious lion.

The book should have broad appeal given the popularity of both the sci-fi and the fantasy genres today. It combines action and adventure, with a light-hearted tone. I have also written another story which takes place in the same magical world, though each story can stand-alone, since the series creates a succession of adventures within this world with a focus on different characters.

I was inspired to write this book while working as a junior high school teacher and letting my imagination soar in my free time.

I would be glad to submit some sample chapters, the complete manuscript, or illustrations for further review, and I look forward to hearing from you.

Sincerely,

SAMPLE LETTERS FOR SCREENPLAYS

Subject Line: Comedy about a man searching for a break who gets his wish with unexpected and hilarious results

Dear***********:

WISHING is a comedy about a man who starts and fails in starting a series of companies. Then his hopes for a lucky break turn hilarious when he gets a wish—which turns into a series of unexpected mishaps.

Here's the plot in a nutshell. Jim Franklin is a serial entrepreneur, who has tried to start dozens of businesses to become successful. Among them are:

- a coal mining company in which his bumbling actions result in the near collapse of the mine

- a small grocery store in which he is arrested after he buys hot chickens from an undercover cop.

He's trying to follow in the footsteps of his beloved mother who died in a strange ship mishap, but nothing seems to work.

Then, one night, Jim wishes for a little luck in a prayer and suddenly gets a LOT of luck. He now wins at everything, such as when he plays the slots, goes to the races, and plays bridge as a favor to his girlfriend. His luck gradually changes and at first it doesn't affect his relationships.

Then he wins big on a TV game show and the press descends. But the fame and adulation soon begin interfering with his life and relationship with his girlfriend His friends find themselves being shoved aside because of the notoriety and Jim doesn't notice this. And the promise Jim made to his girlfriend to marry if he ever made it doesn't seem as important now. So Jim finds himself with fortune and fame and without the people that meant anything to him. Thus, he decides to escape by spending a few weeks on a tropical island, where he decides to simplify his life and make it what it once was. His hope is that he will now be able to win back his friends and lover, and ultimately, as he fulfills that dream, he feels he truly has gotten what he has wished for all along.

I was inspired to write this script, since like Jim I have started many businesses. Though I haven't been on a game show yet or won any big prize, I'm still hoping—and I'm still starting new businesses. Currently, I'm working in the security industry.

If you're interested, I can send you a more detailed synopsis or a complete script.

Sincerely,

Subject Line: Contemporary drama features an older woman struggling to thrive in the big city after the death of her husband and son.

Dear **********:

SANDRA MULLIGAN is a coming of age story for a 50-year old woman who has lived all her life in a small town and has to adjust to life in the city after the sudden death of her husband, followed by the tragic death of her son. It's a story of human struggle and the search for self-reliance, despite difficult odds, and realizing the need for connecting with others, because Sandra cannot do it alone.

Here's a brief overview of the plot. After Sandra's husband suddenly dies, she leaves the only conservative small town life she has known, to live with her son in his apartment in the big city. But soon after she moves in, her son is tragically killed in a robbery in a shopping center, and now she is alone, continuing to live in her son's apartment. After she makes friends with some other women in their 50s and 60s, she sees how easily they can become the victim of crime, when a good friend and others are assaulted.

As a result of these experiences, she is determined to protect herself by joining a self-defense class and finds herself part of a network of younger independent woman. In addition, she finds a protector in a detective who was originally a friend of her son's, and he matches him with the son of a friend. So eventually she is able to create a strong network of friends in the city, becoming both self-reliant while letting other people in to become an important part of her new life.

The film should have broad appeal to the growing Boomer population, now about 30 million strong. I was inspired to write this script because I can relate to losing my husband and starting over. I want to show what women are up against, and how they are able to empower themselves, and seek ways to meet the challenges of our modern world.

If you're interested, I can send you a more detailed synopsis or the complete script by e-mail or regular mail.

Sincerely,

SAMPLE LETTERS FOR THE SALE OF FILM RIGHTS

Subject Line: Film Rights Available for Newly Published Book about a Woman Who Used Her Skills as an Actress to Survive in World War II

Dear **********:

I'm interested in selling the film rights to my recently published book, ACTOR AND SURVIVOR, THE STORY OF KATIE WILHELM, ACTRESS OF AUSCHWITZ. It's the true story of a woman who used her acting skills to charm the Nazis away, and it has the same broad appeal as films like The Pianist and Life is Beautiful.

Famed throughout Europe as a stage actress, Katie Wilhelm went into hiding after the Nazis invaded Holland but was eventually arrested and sent to Auschwitz. But then she became an actress in the performances used to entertain the captors. Eventually, she caught the attention of top Nazis, who brought her to Daschau to form a stage troupe there. After two years, she was liberated and recruited by the U.S. Army as a Nazi hunter. After the war she resumed her career and went on to become a successful actress on television as well as stage. Despite its dark surroundings, this is an inspirational story about the indisputable power of acting and entertainment and the indefatigable strength of the human spirit.

My book grew out of an article I wrote for the NY Times titled 'Acting Saved Her Life.' I have had extensive experience in writing for both magazines and newspapers, as well as editing copy for several publications, including **********. I own the film rights to this story outright.

I would be willing to travel to talk to any interested party and would be happy to send a copy of the book as well. I look forward to your reply.

Sincerely,

SAMPLE LETTER FOR TV SHOWS

Subject Line: New TV Show Features a Mix of Music, Homes, and Everyday Lifestyles

Dear *********:

I'm looking for an agent to represent my proposed new show—THE HOME STAGE, which features people showing off their families, homes, and favorite type of music. Think of the show like a 30-minute music video, which is composed of a sampling of music of a certain genre, and in the first 15 minutes, people with new homes are featured, and the second 15 minutes, owners with remodeled homes are featured.

The people featured can either be shown in slides or video clips which they send in that are edited together to feature a seamless show, where people show of their homes and families with class. The advertisement on the show is in the form of logo insertions on the slides or video clips or featured homes and real estate agents that are advertised. The show begins with a voice-over of me welcoming the audience to THE HOME STAGE and the music being featured tonight (ie: HOME STAGE Pop or HOME STAGE R&B). Then, the rest of the show is the collage of slides or videos as the music plays, and as the show closes, I invite people to send in their photos or video clips for consideration for a future show.

The show can be a great vehicle for advertising and promotion, based on advertising homes, real estate agents, or home products through logo insertions. Individual shows can also be tailored to specific markets on cable TV stations that are targeted to particular groups of people or regions of the country. It is a format that can be targeted to give advertisers any demographic they want in choosing the type of music, homes, and participants to be featured.

My own background in developing the show is as a real estate agent and home staging company owner. And I have long sought to give people what they want, which is what led me to create this show.

Would you like to learn more? I can send you a more detailed proposal, along a few minutes of video to show how these slides and video clips might be melded together to create a unique, compelling new show.

Sincerely,

Subject Line: Inspirational TV Show Features Interviews with People Who Have Survived Major Disasters

Dear ************

THE WINNING EDGE is an inspirational program which shows how those who have survived disasters can be an inspiration to others. They can help others face the aftermath of a disaster or other ordinary problems and take control of their lives. Also, it will appeal to the millions of viewers who like viewing the difficulties of others and seeing them overcome their problems.

The show will take place in front of a live audience with several different people being interviewed on each show, plus cut-aways to show people facing a disaster and successfully coping with the aftermath. The format of the show will feature different types of disaster categories, such as surviving:

• hurricanes

• shark attacks

• mine cave-ins

• ski accidents

• auto crashes

• a serious disease

The show categories are endless. The premise of the show is although most of us face disasters or have family members or friends who have done so, viewing others surviving and overcoming similar situations can help others recover and gain success in life. As the show illustrates, though we may feel we are in it alone and cannot recover the life we once knew, others in similar circumstances have found the courage to fight and not become a victim. Then, their success in getting through the problem may inspire others to similarly fight to overcome their problem and develop a positive life-affirming attitude. The show will accordingly feature short interviews with viewers who have succeeded in overcoming their problems as a result of seeing the show.

I have been inspired to develop this show through my own experiences, in which I have found a way to overcome some terrible crises, look for the good in the bad, and gain the inspiration to move forward. In turn, these tough times have led me to want to inspire and help others get through what may seem like the toughest time of their life.

As for me, I'm 30, live in London, and I have overcome my parents' tragic death in a car accident when I was 4, an aunt's suicide when I was 14, and losing my leg in a ski accident when I was 20. Though I coped with a deep depression and could only manage working in a factory for awhile, after numerous jobs and some help from a supportive minister, I came to run my own multi-million dollar corporation employing 35-40 staff members. It grew from a small dress design business in my garage.

Would you like to learn more? I can send you a more detailed description of the TV show in Word, text, rtf, or PDF format or mail this to you, as you prefer.

Sincerely,

SAMPLE LETTER FOR
ARTICLES AND COLUMNS

Subject Line: Column for Syndication Published in 8 LA Newspapers Based on Taking Car Trips to Offbeat Places

Dear ************:

OFF THE BEATEN TRACK is a weekly column, now published in 8 papers in the L.A. area, which provides a fun, adventurous way to go on adventures in your car. Not your traditional travel column, OFF THE BEATEN TRACK features a varied format of interesting places to go, interviews with people living there, and historical and contemporary anecdotes. The column covers topics such as: a town that had it's own pied piper, a tour of haunted houses and interviews with a ghost hunter, a back-stage look at a stage company, all treated with a light-hearted approach. I have included a sample column at the end of this query letter, and can send you others by e-mail or regular mail.

I bring an extensive background in travel. Besides being a travel agent, I have taught classes on travel and led a program on how to travel on a shoe string, which attracted thousands of participants over the past five years. I have also written hundreds of articles about travel for local newspapers and travel magazines.

Currently my column reaches a weekly readership of about 1.2 million readers in the L.A. area, including these papers: ***********. I would be willing to edit my columns to include stories from states all over the U.S. to fit the states where the column runs. I am also available to assist with other marketing strategies to promote my column.

I look forward to discussing the possibilities for this column with you further, and can send you additional columns by e-mail or regular mail. You can see a sample column below.

Sincerely,

And here's a sample column:

SAMPLE COLUMN GOES HERE

Made in the USA